Author's Note

This book contains folk stories and descriptions of traditions and cultural practices. China is a diverse country with many variations in how these are passed along. Only a few of China's dynasties are included in this book.

Dedication

Thank you to my wonderful daughters, who gave me the excuse to travel to China and fall in love with their birth country, and to my husband for his unwavering support. This book is dedicated to them. —Allison

This book is dedicated to Meg, Nick and Mia. —Lin

Acknowledgments

I want to thank all the people who have helped and encouraged me along this journey from the Sacramento Chinese Culture Foundation, the Organization of Chinese Americans and Families with Children from China. A special shout out to Amy Lin Tan, PhD, as well as Ann Martin Bowler, who wrote the first book in this series, *All About Korea*. Han Moy prepared the instructions for brush painting and calligraphy. Lili Lee contributed the almond jello recipe. Zack Lee prepared all the early illustrations for the crafts. —Allison

How to Pronounce Vowels and Consonants in Mandarin

Mandarin is China's official language, although other dialects are spoken. Pinyin uses the alphabet to show how to pronounce the characters. This table shows the main Mandarin sounds which are not found in English.

MANDARIN	APPROX ENGLISH EQUAL	SAMPLE WORD	EXCEPTION
q	ch	chin	
r	ur	pleasure	
x	Sh	she	
zh	j	urge	
z	ds	birds	
ai	eye	lie	
ao	ow	how	
e	ur	turn	
ei	ay	may	
o	aw	drop	
oo	too	too	
ou	oh	low	
ui	ay	way	
i	ee	tree	
i	ir	Sir	If 'i' follows zh, ch, shi, z, c, s

On the Cover

The small piece of art in the lower right corner next to Lin Wang's name is called a "seal," which is an artist's signature. These can be found on all traditional scroll art, calligraphy, and most modern art. Most Chinese seals have the artist's name, as well as a saying or picture that says something about them as a person, such as their philosophy.

All About
CHINA
Stories, Songs, Crafts
and Games for Kids

ALLISON "AIXIN" BRANSCOMBE

Illustrated by
LIN WANG

TUTTLE Publishing

Tokyo | Rutland, Vermont | Singapore

Contents

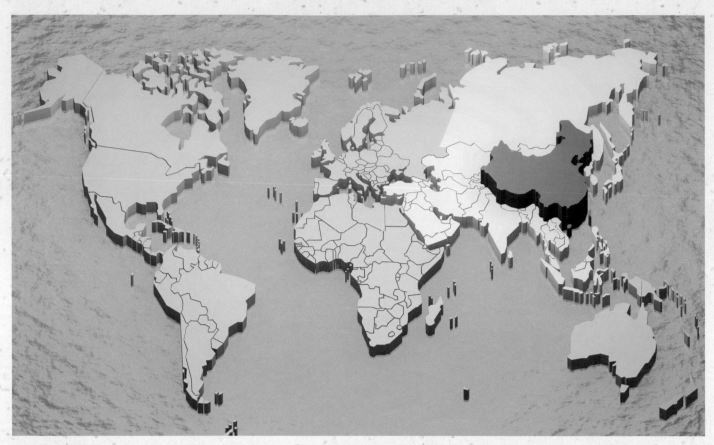

Introducing China

China's Place in the World

Nihao! 你好!

That means Hello! My name is Meiling. You can say "May-ling." My cousin Liming ("Lee Ming") and I will travel with you in China, our country. We live in an amazing culture, where the people share centuries-old traditions and beliefs.

When some people look at China on a map, they see a rooster, with the head to the northeast (upper right), and the vast areas of the southwest as the rooster's wings, body, and tail. To the southeast, the rooster's breast is the heart of China. Different climates around China result in big differences in how people live, what they eat and their daily activities.

China is modernizing very fast, with new technology and fast-growing cities. It is a complicated blend of old and new ways. Let us explore China together! We hope you fall in love with it!

Fast Facts

China was named the People's Republic of China (PRC) in 1949.

China is the world's longest continuous civilization, lasting over 5,000 years. Many inventions we use today came from China—learn about them beginning on page 13.

China has the world's biggest population—1.4 billion people. (India is second with 1.2 billion; the United States has only 310 million.) Counting Chinese people living outside of China, about one in four people in the entire world is Chinese.

China is a country on the continent of Asia. About half the world's population are Asian.

All the world's major religions are practiced in China, including Buddhism, Taoism, Islam, and Christianity. Only Taoism began in China, the others came from outside.

The highest and lowest points in the world are in China. Every ecosystem is in China—including lakes, glaciers, deserts, mountains, coral reefs, rivers, grassland, and tropical rainforests.

About half of China's people live in cities and half live in rural areas and villages.

China's many minority groups have different ways of dressing for special occasions. About 92 percent of Chinese people are from the Han ethnic group, and 8 percent are from 55 different minority groups, which contribute to China's wonderful diversity.

○ China's minority groups have many different ways of dressing. Look at the kids to the left. What do you notice? Can you describe the ways that their clothing is different?

A Tour of China's Famous Historic Places

Amazing Structures, Natural Wonders, and Sights

⊙ Terra-cotta soldiers guarding Qin Shi Huang's Tomb in Xian, Shaanxi

⊙ The Qinghai Mosque is a center for Islamic worship and studies in Urumqi, Xinjiang.

⊙ The Potala Palace, a sacred palace in Lhasa, Tibet, is the former home of the Dalai Lama.

⊙ The Yellow Crane Tower is in Wuhan, Hubei.

⊙ The world-famous Wolong Panda Reserv is in Chengdu, Sichua

Mount Everest on the Tibetan Plateau is also called Chomolungma, or "Holy Mother," in Tibetan; its Chinese name is Shengmu Feng, meaning "Divine Mother Peak." ⊙

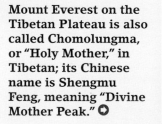

⊙ A lovely home overlooks the amazing Shilin Stone Forest in Kunming, Yunnan.

⊙ The water and mountains provide great contrasts on the beautiful Li River and Guilin Mountains in Guangxi.

The Summer Palace in Beijing is on a beautiful lake.

Tiananmen Square is the gateway to the Forbidden City in Beijing.

A man admires a dragon ice sculpture at the Harbin Festival of Ice and Snow in Heilongjiang Province.

The Great Wall, originally about 5,300 miles long. It can be seen from space!

The Mid-Air Temple, Datong, Shanxi looks like it is hanging in space!

Suzhou Gardens, in Jiangsu

Intricately detailed Tengwang Pavilion, in Nanchang, Jiangxi

Taoist Ancestral Temple, in Foshan, Guangdong

A sampan floats lazily in Victoria Harbor, Hong Kong.

Visit Taiwan's National Palace Museum.

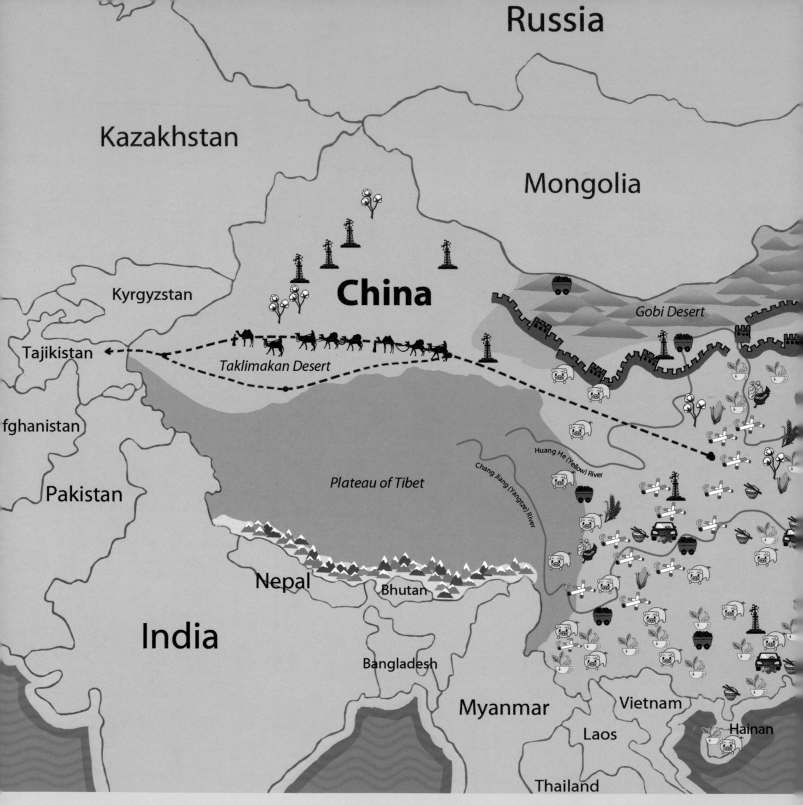

A Look At China's Geography

Everyone knows China produces rice, but did you know that China is the world's biggest producer of cotton, tea, pork, wheat, and tobacco? Lots of farms raise ducks, and chickens too. Since most Chinese people do not have cow's milk, cheese or beef, dairy farms are uncommon. Lots of electricity is produced by coal, water, and more recently, by solar and wind farms. China makes many more things than this map can show.

Legend

- = silk
- = manufacturing
- = electronics
- = oil fields
- = tobacco
- = tea
- = cotton
- = corn
- = wheat
- = pig farm
- = coal
- = rice
- = Great Wall
- - - - - = Silk Road
- = Grand Canal

North Korea

South Korea

Yellow Sea

Japan

East China Sea

Taiwan

outh hina ea

Philippines

N

W   E

S

China is a land of contrasts. See if you can find all these regions: In the **northwest** are deserts, glaciers, and very tall mountains; in the **northeast**, there are more mountains and forests with bone-chilling winters. In the **south** and **southeast** are the fertile lowlands where China grows the food needed to feed its people and to trade with the rest of the world; in the **southwest** are the high mountain plateaus of the Tibetan region. Can you guess how much of China's land can actually be used for growing food? It is a very small amount—only 12 percent. Can you find where the melting snow of the Himalayas creates the Chang Jiang and Huang He rivers? They are the third and sixth longest rivers in the world.

China's Government

中国 The Chinese character for China means "middle kingdom." Why? Long ago, Chinese people believed China was the center of the world. Today, China has 22 provinces, plus five autonomous regions like Tibet, created for minority groups, four separate big cities (Shanghai, Beijing, Chongqing, and Tianjin), plus Hong Kong and Macau.

◐ This is the Great Hall of the People in Beijing where the National People's Congress meets.

The National People's Congress elects China's President (Xi Jinping in 2013), and the President of the Supreme People's Court. The people of China do not elect their leaders. The laws and programs carried out in China are developed and approved by the Communist Party, and enforced locally by people appointed by the Party.

China's money is called the renminbi, or RMB for short. A common unit of RMB is the yuan. ◐

人民币

Did you know Taiwan was originally part of China? In 1949, Taiwan separated from China, keeping China's name (the Republic of China, or ROC), while mainland China became the People's Republic of China, or PRC. Like two arguing brothers, Taiwan and China disagree over whether or not Taiwan should still be a part of China. Perhaps one day they will find a way to coexist in harmony. Taiwan is bustling with growth, just like China.

China's Favorite Folk Song

"Mo Li Hua" means "Jasmine Flowers"

Composed during the reign of Emperor Qianlong (1735–1796), *Mo Li Hua* has been performed on many important occasions, including the opening of the 2008 Olympic Games in Beijing.

Mò Lì Huā 茉莉花

hǎo yī duǒ měi lì de mò lì huā hǎo yī duǒ měi lì de mò lì huā
jasmine flower, oh so fair, jasmine flower, oh so fair
好 一 朵 美 丽 的 茉 莉 花 好 一 朵 美 丽 的 茉 莉 花

fēn fāng měi lì mǎn zhī yá yòu xiāng yòu bái rén rén kuā
budding and blooming here and there, pure and fragrant all declare
芬 芳 美 丽 满 枝 桠 又 香 又 白 人 人 夸

ràng wǒ lái jiāng nǐ zhāi xià sòng gěi bié rén jiā
let me take you with tender care, your sweetness for all to share
让 我 来 将 你 摘 下 送 给 别 人 家

mò lì huā ya mò lì huā mò lì huā ya mò lì huā
jasmine flower, oh jasmine flower jasmine flower oh jasmine flower
茉 莉 花 呀 茉 莉 花 茉 莉 花 呀 茉 莉 花

The Legend of Pan Gu 盘古开天辟地的神话
How the Earth Came To Be

Before Earth existed, a giant egg floated in the vast universe. Inside was a jumble of yin and yang, the foundation of life, and a powerful giant, Pan Gu, who was waking up from a sleep of thousands of years.

"Where am I?" roared Pan Gu. "I will build a new world from this yin and yang. I will create women and men who will know sadness and joy, and eat food that is both bitter and sweet, so they may live a full life." Out of the shell he made the sky, Earth, mountains, and valleys. His breath became the wind and clouds. As he passed away, his blood became the oceans and rivers, his eyes became the moon and the sun, and his hair turned into trees, flowers, birds, animals, insects, and of course, people.

"I love this world—the sweet melodies of the birds, the fragrant smells of the flowers and the harmonious ways of the people," proclaimed Nu Wa, a beautiful goddess who came down to Earth.

One day two gods had a big fight, causing it to rain so hard the sky collapsed. Nu Wa pushed a huge stone into the hole where the flood waters poured in, adding colorful stones from the seas, rivers, and lakes. She wrapped the stones with all the vines, bamboo, and reeds she could find. At last, the rain and the floods stopped and the sun appeared again.

"I have defeated the quarreling gods and saved Earth's rich resources, its people, and the creations of Pan Gu," said Nu Wa. And she was glad that the yin and yang remained for all time.

5,000 Years of Culture and Inventions

The earliest Chinese people lived along the Huang He (Yellow) River, beginning more than 12,000 years ago during the Neolithic Period according to archeologists—so long ago! Legend says that Huang Di, the Yellow Emperor, is the common ancestor of all Chinese people. So many things we use today were invented by the Chinese. How many do you know about?

About 2600 BCE, it is said that Huang Di created the lunar calendar and the zodiac. People also figured out a way to record time, as no one had clocks then! They also created a standard counting system using multiples of 10, and an early form of writing.

夏朝 Xia Dynasty (2070–1600 BCE)

Over 3,500 years ago in the Xia Dynasty, they grew rice, corn, tea, and soybeans, and made pottery and copper objects. Chopsticks were in use even then!

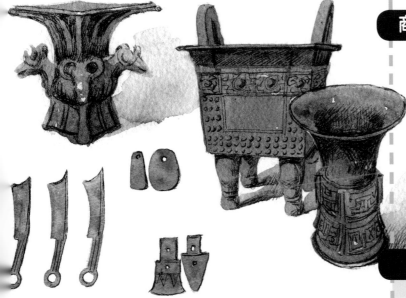

商朝 Shang Dynasty (1600–1046 BCE)

◐ China became the most skilled bronze-working civilization in the world, as people heated, melted, and cast metal to make pots, pans, tools, weapons, and household items. How were things preserved? People found that painting lacquer (tree sap) on wood protected it from water, bugs, and decay. Beginning about 1300 BCE, lacquer was painted on wood, houses, bowls, furniture, and ships. This allowed ancient things to survive for centuries, helping archeologists to see how people lived so long ago.

周朝 Zhou Dynasty (1046–256 BCE)

Around 400 BCE, huge blast furnaces were invented to melt the iron out of iron ore, 1,200 years before this happened in Europe. It was now possible to make extra big pots, tools, and sculptures of gods.

◑ In the last of the ancient dynasties, the Zhou Dynasty, people invented clever ways to bring water to crops—called irrigation systems—to grow ever larger amounts of food. Planting and irrigating crops in rows came about in this period. Over the centuries, Chinese agricultural methods became world famous, being adopted and used around the world today.

秦朝 Qin ("Ch'in") Dynasty (221–206 BCE)

China's name, meaning "Middle Kingdom," comes from the Qin Dynasty, which Europeans used to pronounce as "Chine." Powerful Emperor Qin Shihuang ruled from 221 to 206 BCE. In only 15 years he created standardized coins, weights and measures for use in trading, and built roads and canals linking the provinces with the capital. Qin imposed heavy taxes to pay for these huge projects.

The Dujiangyan Irrigation System was an engineering wonder! It stopped flooding, and channeled the Minjiang River to provide water for farming on the Chengdu Plain, now known as China's breadbasket. Built in 223 BCE, this irrigation system still operates today.

◐ Qin Shihuang built one of the most elaborate tombs known to mankind. Guarding his underground tomb were the Terra-cotta Warriors—8,000 life-size soldiers, all made of clay. Each one wore different clothes, with a different face, nose, eyes, hair, and armor. Many rode horses or chariots and held real bronze weapons. Qin had the tombs booby-trapped to stop grave robbers, so archeologists did not discover these underground warriors until 1974!

汉朝 Han Dynasty (206 BCE–220 CE)

Emperor Wu Di sent Zhang Qian to central Asia to make friends with China's enemies, primarily the Huns. This was the start of the "Silk Road" trade route, along which China's beautiful silks, lacquer ware, porcelain, tea, and spices were exported. The Silk Road (shown on page 8), started a network of trade routes linking China, India, Europe, and the Middle East.

◐ How did the Great Wall come about? Started in small sections by previous rulers, it was built up and extended in the Qin Dynasty to keep out invading tribes from the north. Engineers designed a way to link shorter walls with deep, strong foundations. Ultimately, it stretched for thousands of miles across northern China. About one million workers, soldiers, and prisoners labored for many, many years. Thousands died in the effort.

The Chinese invented the wheelbarrow, called the wooden ox, which made carrying big loads easier. This was also the first rickshaw, where one person pulls one or two people on a small platform.

Engineers designed deep mine shafts allowing China to mine coal, salt, and iron ore. The first suspension bridges allowed people to cross rivers and canyons. Around 100 CE, the first calculator was invented, called the abacus, along with the first seismograph, to detect earthquakes.

Top to bottom: Seismograph (Han Dynasty), magnetic compass (Song Dynasty), and abacus (Han Dynasty). ◐

14

隋朝 Sui Dynasty (581–617 CE)

A huge engineering feat was completed during the Sui Dynasty: the 1,114 mile (1,792 km) long Grand Canal linked the Huang He and Chang Jiang rivers. Still heavily used, it carried huge barges and small sampans with silk, coal, food, and factory goods from north to south. Compare the Grand Canal to the Suez Canal (120 miles/193 km) and the Panama Canal (about 51 miles/82 km). Can you find the Grand Canal on page 9?

唐朝 Tang Dynasty (618–907 CE)

The Tang Dynasty is called the Golden Age of China. Printed books with poetry and literature became commonly available for people to read. Over the years, experiments with porcelain glazes on pottery led to what became "fine china" in the Song Dynasty. Paper money was invented so tax collectors did not need to carry coins.

The new practice of foot binding made women more obedient to men, and made it painful to walk. Except for those who worked in fields, most women had bound feet. Adult women's feet were about the size of a 3–5 year old child—exquisite silk embroidered shoes hid their tiny broken feet. Footbinding continued until it was banned in the late 1800s-early 1900s.

○ **The world's first mechanical clock made by Yi Xiang in 725. It was huge—see the person on the top left platform!**

Did you know that the oldest piece of paper was found in a Chinese tomb around 86 BCE (2,100 years ago)? It was made from bark and rope fibers, then strengthened with bamboo. This was different from ancient Egyptian paper made from papyrus.

宋朝 Song Dynasty (960–1279 CE)

By the time of the Song Dynasty, China had over 100 million people. These inventions forever changed the world:

- Magnetic compasses made ocean travel possible.
- Spinning wheels wove fibers into thread, boosting silk and cotton making.
- The "rainbow" bridge design helped tall boats use rivers.
- Chinese printing machines spurred communication; improved kilns and pottery molds created delicate porcelain.
- Chemists developed gunpowder, which led to the later invention of guns and rockets.
- Daoist monks developed the first vaccine against a dreaded disease, small pox.

During the Song Dynasty, fine dining became possible with the invention of the wok, while fine teas were sipped from beautiful porcelain china cups. Fancy restaurants and inns spread to serve traveling merchants. These new ways made the bustling cities of China even friendlier. How often do you and your family go to a restaurant or hotel?

元朝 Yuan Dynasty (1271–1368 CE)

Ghenghis Khan created the Mongol Empire in central Asia and Europe through military battles. His grandson, Kublai Khan, founded the Yuan Dynasty. The Yuan Dynasty was the first and only Mongol-controlled dynasty. As trade flourished along the Silk Road, many people of Muslim faith moved to China and brought new cultural influences from central Asia, influencing lifestyle, food, and household furnishings.

⬆ **Where are the pillars of the "rainbow" bridge? The genius of the design was that none were needed to hold it up! Now tall boats could use so many more rivers.**

明朝 Ming Dynasty (1368–1644 CE)

Under the Ming Dynasty, exquisite arts and crafts flourished, and the Great Wall was repaired and extended. A grand period of exploration occurred after Ming Emperor Zhu Di directed hundreds of ships to be built and filled with expensive jewelry, silks, tea, and other goods to trade with the world. Named "The Treasure Fleet," 317 ships carrying 27,000 men (including cooks, doctors, scribes, priests, and diplomats), sailed south into the open sea in 1405. Commanded by Admiral Zheng He, they visited 37 countries.

These inventions helped the Treasure Fleet take seven trips across open seas instead of hugging coastlines, which is risky:

- Paper and printing were used to make long paper sailing charts. Reading from the magnetic compass helped to calculate star locations and length of time for travel.

- Moveable rudders, invented in the Han Dynasty, steered these big sailing ships.
- Moveable sails meant sailors did not have to wait for winds to blow in the right direction.

Sadly, after Zheng He returned, civil wars halted new trips. Many journals from his voyages were lost. Some think he may have reached America and Australia, but proof is hard to find. Still, China's role as a powerful maritime trader began with the travels of Zheng He's fleet.

⊕ During the Ming Dynasty, the process of mass-producing exquisite blue and white porcelain was developed. This beautiful house ware became known as "fine china" around the world.

⊕ Two amazing buildings were built in Beijing during the Ming dynasty: The Temple of Heaven (above) and the Imperial Palace. Both were built of wood—without using any nails!

The Imperial Palace was known as the Forbidden City, because it was off limits to everyone but royalty, their families, servants and staff, and people on official business. Now a world-class museum, about 9,000 people lived there during the Ming and Qing dynasties.

The Temple of Heaven was where the Emperor went to pray in winter for an abundant spring harvest.

⊕ ⊕ Can you imagine sailing across an ocean and all you can see is endless miles of waves? Can you imagine making friends with strangers who don't speak your language? How would you go about it? Would you bring gifts or weapons?

The first 150 years of the Qing Dynasty were its glory days. China now stretched from Manchuria (the rooster's head on pages 8-9) to Mongolia, Central Asia (parts of what is now Kazakhstan and Kyrgyzstan); south to Tibet and Southeast Asia, including parts of what is now Vietnam, Laos, Cambodia, Myanmar, and Thailand. Demand grew for Chinese goods. For example in 1684, tea traders began to sell to England. In 1720, they sold 400,000 pounds of tea; by 1800, this grew to 23 million pounds! Other Chinese-made goods like

● In 1908, three-year old Pu Yi became China's last emperor, ending China's Imperial Period. Under an agreement with the new government, Pu Yi stopped being emperor in 1912, but was allowed to live in the Inner Court. After being the home of 24 emperors during the Ming and Qing dynasties, the Forbidden City was no longer the political center of China.

● This Marble Boat and the Summer Palace (page 7) were lavishly restored by Empress Dowager Cixi. She took money meant for building a strong navy. Without this, several coastal cities were taken over by other countries. One was Hong Kong, which was not returned to China until 1997.

● In Imperial China, the dragon symbolized yang, the power and majesty of the emperor, and the phoenix symbolized yin, the feminine qualities of the empress. Today, the dragon is still a symbol of power, wealth, and respect. Did you know the dragon of royalty had five claws, while the people's dragon had only three or four? Traditionally, colors had special meanings:
• Red was for happiness, worn at weddings and on festive holidays.
• Yellow was for royalty. In ancient times, only emperors and empresses could wear yellow. Common people could be jailed (or worse!) for wearing yellow.
• Green symbolized spring and renewal.
• White was traditionally worn when people mourned a death.
• Dark blue and black were worn as common people's working clothes.

silk, porcelain, cotton and cloisonné (page 42) were in great demand around the world.

But the last half of the 1800s was quite difficult. Millions died in the Taiping Rebellion (a civil war), floods and droughts. A series of humiliating defeats by other countries forced China to give up land: in the Opium War, Hong Kong was ceded to the British. The Anglo-French invasion, also called the Second Opium War, the Sino-Japanese War, and the Boxer Rebellion, which led to the Eight Nation Alliance War, also caused big land losses. Revolutionary forces led by Sun Yat-Sen overthrew the Qing Dynasty and formed the Republic of China in 1911.

Because living conditions were so hard in the late 1800s due to floods, drought and war, many thousands moved to California (called "Gold Mountain") in the United States. They worked in gold mines, on the Transcontinental Railroad, and built levees in the Sacramento Delta, to channel water to grow crops. Many sent back their wages to help pay for Sun Yat-Sen's revolution to end China's dynasties. Today, Sun Yat-Sen is known as the Father of New China.

In 1937, an eight year war started when Japan invaded China—their bombs killed many people and destroyed precious historic buildings and ancient treasures. In 1941, American volunteers formed the Flying Tigers Air Squadron, to support China in its fight against Japan. After Japan attacked Pearl Harbor in 1941, the United States entered World War II, and China and the US supported each other.

In 1946, fights between Mao Zedong's Communists and Generalissimo Chiang Kai-Shek's Nationalist Army, called the Kuomintang, led to a three-year civil war. In the end, Chiang fled to Taiwan, keeping China's name (the Republic of China, or

○ In the 1990s, construction of the Three Gorges Dam began. For centuries, the Chang Jiang River overflowed its banks during rainy seasons, causing thousands to die or be made homeless. The dam controls this powerful river and creates electric energy for China's industries to grow.

ROC). Mao Zedong renamed the mainland the People's Republic of China (PRC) on October 1, 1949.

More recently, hosting the 2008 Summer Olympics in Beijing was a great success. Preparing for the Olympics helped China modernize many facilities and spurred rapid growth. Chinese athletes won many medals. Putting on such a successful international event brought national pride and glory to China that will not be forgotten.

Sun Yat-Sen, Chiang Kai-Shek and Mao Zedong

Home Sweet Home

What do you think it is like to live in one of these homes?

Since the earliest times, farmers used walls to protect their homes and land. Massive walls surrounded ancient Chinese cities. In fact, towns grew inside Chinese walls. Regardless of the outside appearance, many people in rural or suburban China live in simple two or three room homes. The extended family sleeps and cooks together. Cooking is done on a simple wood or coal-fired stove in the center of the home. Following are six less common, and very unusual types of homes.

○ In cold northern China, families sleep on platform beds, called *kangs*, which sometimes use flues to carry heat from the stove to underneath the bed for warmth.

○ Homes are built on a north–south axis with only one entrance, and no windows on the outside walls. This gives great privacy, as well as protection from winds, sandstorms, and strangers. When you look in through the main entrance, most homes have a free-standing wall to block the view into the home for the family's privacy. Many families believe this wall blocks evil spirits from entering the home, as evil spirits only move in a straight line. Stone lions guard this home.

○ *Hutongs* are narrow lanes and alleys that wind and twist through older sections of cities like Beijing. Homes of three or four rooms crowd in between low-rise courtyard walls. These courtyard houses within a big city often share outside toilets and water. They are filled with crooked alleyways, where you might see kids playing or people selling fruits and vegetables. *Hutongs* date back about 800 years. As you drive around older parts of Beijing, you may see communities living in *hutongs*, but high-rise apartments are fast replacing them.

○ As you can see here, the courtyard design has been used for many centuries. The size depends on the wealth of the family. Usually, several families live together, with grandparents, aunts, uncles, and children. There is always an inner courtyard, and sometimes several separate inner courtyard spaces for family ceremonies, pens for animals, and gardens for relaxation or growing food.

○ In Fujian in southeast China you can see Hakka apartment buildings that look like giant round or square donuts! Home for 20–100 families, they have no downstairs windows on the outside, and only one entrance that is easy to close. Inside are the community area, play area, and garden, all open to the sky. Doesn't this look like a safe place for children, who can be watched by adults everywhere?

○ The famous Forbidden City was a true city within a city, separated from the rest of Beijing. Thousands of people lived inside its four walls. It was built between 1407 and 1420, totally without nails! Behind its high, red walls and moats were 800 beautiful halls and temples, set among gardens, courtyards, and bridges. It housed 9,999 rooms—a lucky Chinese number. In the 1700s, about 9,000 people lived there. Over a period of 600 years, 24 different emperors lived here, set apart from their people. Ordinary Chinese people were not even allowed to approach its gates! The Forbidden City is also known as the Imperial Palace. It is the largest palace in the world!

Although Chinese cities are growing rapidly, about half of China's people still live in rural areas and villages. These villages give people their sense of identity and sense of home. When introducing themselves, Chinese people typically name the village from which their family came, even if they moved away long ago. Those who have moved far away from their villages, or even outside of China, often go on "root-seeking" tours to their ancestral villages, and trace their heritage back for centuries.

While a small (but increasing) percentage of families have electric washers in their apartments, most families hang their clothes out to dry on their balconies. Can you imagine this very colorful sight, to see many patterns of clothes, blowing in the wind? What do you think the children and grandfather are talking about in this typical city apartment? ⊙

⊙ Cool in summer and warm in winter, these cave dwellings in northern Shaanxi Province are dug out of a thick, yellow soil called loess, using simple hand tools.

In Tibet, multistory homes are built into the sides of steep mountains. In the Himalayan Mountains, Tibet's winters are among the coldest on earth. The family's animals stay on the lowest level, so the warmth of their bodies rises to help heat the floors above. ⊙

⊙ Yurts are round tents used by Mongolian and Kazak nomads who move with their horses, sheep, goats, and yaks across cold grasslands. Made of animal skins and blankets, they are mounted on wood frames and are easily taken down, moved, and put back up. These can be found in Inner Mongolia and Xinjiang.

Feng Shui Your Bedroom

Have you entered a room where you instantly felt good? Have you been in a room where you felt distracted and found it hard to concentrate? If you answered "yes" to either question, you may be sensitively tuned to the art of feng shui (pronounced "fung shway"). Feng shui is a way to lay out furniture, windows, and doors, and use colors, fabrics, and plants in bedrooms, homes, gardens, and offices to feel happier and healthier.

Feng shui teaches that the earth, just like the human body, has channels of energy carrying good influences. If the channels of energy (qi) are blocked, it can have harmful or negative consequences, such as making us sick or causing problems in our life. If it flows easily, it brings relaxation, and helps us feel good, which makes it easier to study, work and meet our goals.

Here are some simple rules for children's bedrooms. Does your room fit these rules? What would you change?

- Try not to put the head of the bed directly under a window.
- Place the bed so you can look out the windows and also see the bedroom door.
- While in bed, you should not directly face the door, or have the door next to the headboard.

Please note: If you cannot meet these rules, do not worry—there are many ways to work around these rules so the energy in the room can be calm and peaceful. (See Resources, page 62.)

While there were no televisions, computers, or cell phones when feng shui was first developed, we now know these create lots of electronic stimulation, "squashing" the good yin energy in a room. This, plus clutter, creates brain stress, making it hard to relax and sleep peacefully. Modern feng shui books recommend turning off or covering all electronic devices in your bedroom to reduce the amount of bouncing, distracting energy. ⦾

⦾ Do the adults in your life tell you to clean up your room? Beside the fact that it looks better, this suggestion is good feng shui! Clutter in a room—on desks, on the floor, under the bed—blocks the flow of positive energy, allowing the negative energy to build up. Bedrooms should be restful, in order for the quiet yin energy to flow. Colors should be muted—cool or pastel colors to help you sleep. Too much bright or hot color makes it harder to relax.

Daily Life in China
中国人的日常生活

Shopping

High-rise department stores arrange sales areas by type of goods. A whole floor may be devoted to hundreds of independent sellers—mostly women— offering jewelry such as jade, pearls, gold and silver bracelets, necklaces, and earrings. On another floor you might see dozens of purse sellers, and small kitchen appliances like woks and rice cookers on another. Washers, dryers, and refrigerators might be on another floor. Other floors might sell computers and electronics, another with children's clothes, and on another, home decorations such as vases, jade carvings, and sculptures. Can you imagine this? It sure makes it easier to compare prices!

○ In both urban and rural shopping areas, families often live upstairs and have a store downstairs, in buildings called shophouses. Some are specialized, so on certain streets only kitchen goods are sold, others where fresh vegetables and fruits are sold, and yet other streets where just children's clothes are sold, and so on.

China's outdoor markets are a visual feast! These markets are huge, covering acres of land. Hundreds of sellers are organized by type of goods, such as purses, jewelry, herbs, food, fish, flowers, animals, school supplies, and furniture. Whatever you can imagine you would want to buy, you can usually find in at an outdoor market! Be ready to haggle—everyone argues over what price to pay. ○

Making a Living and Getting to Work

China's jobs are probably a lot like the jobs in your country, with teachers, store and bank workers, restaurant owners, scientists and more. In the factories of China's cities, everything imaginable is made, including household appliances, electronics, cars, toys, silk rugs and clothes, and ships. China's economy is the second biggest in the world after the United States. Lots of people work in energy development, such as coal mines and oil fields. Solar and wind farms are appearing on China's landscape, too. Check out the map on pages 8 and 9!

Before the 1980s, workers in China's many government-owned businesses were guaranteed jobs for life. This is no longer the case. Many families need two jobs to earn enough money to feed their families. There is pressure to purchase things like cell phones, computers, televisions, and vehicles. People are moving from the countryside to the big cities, where they hope to get better jobs.

○ Everyone knows about China's rice and tea plantations. Did you know that cotton, wheat, corn, millet, tobacco and soybeans are also farmed, and pigs, ducks, and chickens raised? However, you will not see many dairy farms, since most Chinese people do not eat cheese or beef, or drink milk.

We used to think of China as being a nation of bicycle riders, but this sure has changed! In cities today, people drive motorcycles and cars. Many big cities have subways, while buses are used everywhere, and trains link places far apart. There are several types of trains, including "hard sleepers" and "soft sleepers." Soft sleepers are the most luxurious, including fold-out beds for overnight travel.

High-speed rail has become more common as China leads the way with the greatest number of miles of high speed rail in the world. See the bullet train zipping along above the bikes, busses, trucks and cars stuck in traffic! ○

Current Ways of Dressing

○ This woman wears a red *qipao*, while the man wears a mandarin jacket.

The traditional dress for women, the *qipao* (also commonly called by its Cantonese name, *cheongsam*), is still worn by many women in China and abroad. It is considered China's national dress. The traditional mandarin jacket for men is popular today too.

Working clothes in most businesses and industries are like Western styles of dress, with slacks and shirts or suits for men, and dresses, or slacks or skirts with blouses, for women.

By contrast, farm workers planting and harvesting food wear very simple cotton clothes, which wash easily, and wide-brimmed hats made of straw or bamboo to protect their faces and heads from the hot sun.

The Ancient Silk Industry

While cotton was the fabric for common people, silk was the fabric for emperors and the wealthy. Legend says silk was discovered by Huang Di's wife, Empress Lei Zu around 2500 BCE when she saw silky strands appear after a silk worm's cocoon fell in boiling water. Making fine silk cloth evolved into one of China's earliest industries.

Silkworms eat mulberry tree leaves to create their silk.

The process for making silk was a state secret—revealing the secret was punishable by death, it was so important to China. The secret was kept until about 550 CE, when smugglers hid silkworm larvae in bamboo canes while traveling on the Silk Road. Can you imagine people keeping a secret for nearly 3,000 years?

The name "silk" comes from the Chinese word for silk: *si* ("sih").

Silk production was one of many inventions that made China famous.

Weaving silk on a loom.

A silkworm caterpillar spins a cocoon to protect itself while it becomes a moth. This cocoon is made of continuous, tiny silk threads up to three-quarters of a mile (1.2 km) long, or more! Up to 70 strands of thread are braided into one silk thread. The thread is then put on a special weaving loom and woven into delicate cloth and fine rugs. The spinning wheel and the loom (see left) were invented in China. China's magnificent silk fabrics are valued around the world to this day.

Education

◐ After children start school, many join the Young Pioneers, a civic organization connected with the Communist Party. This is to show they are patriots and want to honor China. The Young Pioneers wear a red scarf around their neck, and also help out with projects to improve the school, like planting trees.

In China, schoolchildren are taught to write their characters over and over, to help them remember so many. The order in which each stroke is drawn is very important to the quality and presentation of the writing—teachers can tell if the stroke order is wrong. ◐

Education

is really valued in our culture! Most kids go to school from ages 6–15, with classes of 50–60 students. Our grandfather walks us to school at 7:30 am and home at 4:30 pm. After junior high school, you must pass a very hard test to get promoted to high school. Students spend hundreds of hours studying to pass their college entrance exam to get into college.

In English, there are 26 letters to learn. Most Chinese need to know 2,500 characters to read a newspaper. Highly educated people know over 5,000!

Chinese Pets

What pets do people keep? Crickets have been pets for thousands of years in China, kept in small cages. Men and women in the Forbidden City carried their crickets in golden cages! People now use bamboo cages. In winter, tiny hot water bottles in the cage keep the crickets warm and happy, so they will sing. Dragonflies are also pets; they are caught and a tiny thread is tied around their waists, making each little dragonfly become a tiny kite, soaring through the air!

Nowadays, families in cities keep fish, birds, dogs, and cats as pets. In a park, you will likely see grandmas and grandpas carrying their birds in cages, so the birds can be near other birds and sing together. Goldfish symbolize wealth and abundance. They are often seen in homes, adding beauty and positive energy to a room.

Let's Have Fun 和我们一起玩

K ids in China play many of the same games that kids all over the world play. Soccer and basketball are two favorites. Children who are especially agile may be chosen for gymnastics or acrobatics school and become performers.

For hours of fun outside, Chinese kids love kite flying, hopscotch, jump rope, spinning toys, walking on stilts, and Chinese yo-yos. *Jianzi*, or "hacky sack," is a game that takes a lot of practice! Try it—it is very fun, but harder than it looks!

○ Chinese yo-yos look like a wooden or plastic hourglass. String is wrapped around the middle and tied to two sticks—then the yo-yo is flicked up, down, back and forth to make it fly high in the air! Practice by yourself, then play with friends, flipping the yo-yo back and forth on the string. Also called diablos, the Chinese yo-yo is believed to be about 4,000 years old!

○ While many people think ping pong was invented in China, the Chinese only took a great game that was invented in Europe in the 1800s and made it their own. It is played all over China, indoors and out.

○ The game of Chinese chess, *xiang chi*, is very popular in Asia. Its rules are quite different from Western chess. The board game is like checkers, but the players move from intersection to intersection, instead of square to square. In a public place, you can often see a crowd gathering around to watch strategy as tiny soldiers, chariots, and elephants move around on the board.

○ Mahjong is also quite popular. It was first played during the Song Dynasty. Four players use 144 tiles. They start out with 16 tiles, then give away what they do not want, while trying to keep tiles that might help their opponents. Mahjong takes skill, planning, and strategy, plus luck. Look in a park with lots of Chinese people and you will see mahjong and Chinese chess played for many hours!

Make Tangram Brain Teasers

Many people know the Chinese invented playing cards, but here is another great indoor game:

Tangrams are seven different shaped pieces made out of a single square. You can make an infinite number of animals, buildings, boats, or people—just use your imagination! According to an old folk tale, tangrams came from a story about little foxes that loved to play tricks on people by changing into different animals. This family game has been popular for centuries—there are many beautiful sets of tangram tiles dating back many years.

See if you can figure out how to arrange the tangram pieces to make the figures below, using only the seven pieces shown on the right. Make up a story about how the animals play together, fool one another, or both! (The solutions are on page 62.)

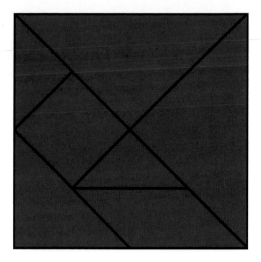

The tangram cutting pattern. Make your own tangram puzzle pieces by tracing this pattern onto a piece of colored paper or cardboard—either as this size, or by enlarging the pieces. All the pieces must stay in the same proportion as shown here. You can color or paste any kind of pattern on the paper to have even more fun.

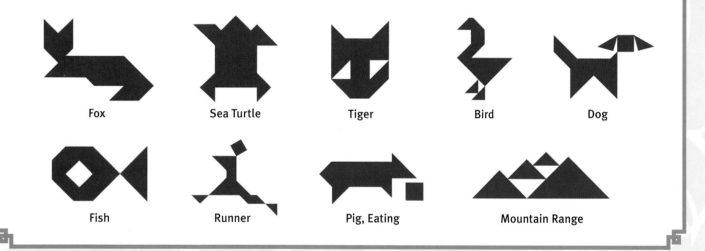

Fox	Sea Turtle	Tiger	Bird	Dog

Fish	Runner	Pig, Eating	Mountain Range

How to Play Jianzi 教你踢毽子

- **Each player keeps a *jianzi*, a lightweight object 3–4 inches (7–10 cm) tall, in the air using just their feet, ankles, knees, and thighs—no hands allowed! Or, several players can share one *jianzi*! This game is like hacky sack.**
- **The first to drop it, loses.**

You can buy *jianzi* at Asian stores, or just use a rolled up sock, a nylon body scrubber, or a pouch of grain. Use your imagination!

Family Traditions and Customs
家庭的传统和习俗

In China, the family name always comes first, and the individual's name is second. Why? It shows the importance of family first, before the individual's identity.

⊙ One month old celebrations and birthdays

When a baby is born, it is considered one year old because of the time it spent growing inside its mother. Historically in China, birthdays were not commonly celebrated until a person reached their 60th year. After that, birthday celebrations came every five years. Long ago, it was rare to live to 60 years old, so this is why the tradition started.

When a baby turns one month old, the family celebrates with a red egg party. Family and friends give toys, clothes, good luck charms, jewelry, and lucky red envelopes with money inside. Chinese legend says that tigers are great protectors of children, so toy tigers are common gifts to newborns. Eggs are dyed red, because red symbolizes happiness and good fortune. What do you think makes the eggs red? They are put in hot water with red envelopes or red beets! New mothers drink ginger and chicken soup to get back energy after giving birth.

Role of Adults

"Filial piety" is a tradition where adult children, particularly the son, take care of their elderly parents. It is considered bad behavior to not care for your frail parents, grandparents, and other elderly relatives.

Role of Grandparents, Elders, and Ancestors

Do your grandparents live with you? Do they live far away? In China, extended families often live together. If you visit a home, you will likely see grandparents caring for their grandchildren, cooking, cleaning, and helping the kids with their homework while the parents are away, sometimes at jobs in other cities. The elderly are respected and treasured as wise people. Adults and children owe them obedience and respect. Many Chinese homes have small altars to honor parents, grandparents, and great grandparents who are no longer living.

Role of Children

A child's job is to study hard in school, and learn all they can for their future employment. They are expected to be helpful to their parents, younger siblings, and elders. In years past, girls were not expected to go to school, or stay in school. They stayed home and helped run the household. Today it is different. Girls attend school, and, just like boys, go as far as possible with their education.

Did you know that when a child is 100 days old, the parents shave its head? This is thought to make the hair grow thicker and more beautiful. This is an ancient tradition that many follow today.

◆ Marriages

Arranged marriages were common in the past, where parents and a matchmaker consult the zodiac to see if the suggested bride and groom were in harmony. Traditionally, the bride and groom did not meet before the wedding. In Western society, people hope to fall in love first and then get married. In Chinese tradition, and other Asian nations, people married first and then fell in love. This made it very important for the parents to find the right match for their son or daughter. Now, parents sometimes still engage a matchmaker to suggest a mate for their child, but the couple do get to know each other before marrying. In China, the married woman goes to live with her husband's family, leaving her birth family behind.

Do you know what "face" means? It is about having the respect and honor of others.

Chinese people have strong feelings of personal pride. Being respected is basic.

- Saving face means protecting your good reputation and avoiding shame or blame.
- Gaining face means others gave you great respect and honor.
- Giving face means you treat others in an honorable or valuable way.
- Losing face means your reputation was hurt, causing embarrassment or shame.
- Arguing or personally attacking someone in public makes them lose face. Negotiate, be diplomatic and give a bit to save face for both sides. Don't bully!

Make Your Own Paper Cutting for "Double Happiness"

Red, the color of happiness, is widely displayed at weddings! The couple on the left is dressed in very traditional wedding outfits with rich, embroidered finery. "Double happiness" is a symbol used in weddings and anniversary celebrations, wishing the newlyweds a long and happy life together.

Enlarge and trace this pattern on a piece of red paper folded in half.

Cut along the black lines, unfold to open out, and then you will have the Chinese characters for "Double Happiness."

Making dim sum is a family activity. Clockwise from top left: *hargow, gow gee, char siu bao* (steamed buns), *shu mai, chun juan* (spring rolls), and *jong* in the center. **O**

Did you know that Chinese noodles were first made from beans and rice flour, beginning about 3,000 years ago? This was one of the foods Marco Polo brought from China to Europe. Now, most noodles are made from wheat or rice. In Italy, long-life noodles are known as spaghetti, of course!

Dim sum is enjoyed all over the world. It is a Cantonese phrase meaning "delicacies that touch the heart." **O**

Food and Eating 饮食文化

In different parts of China, what people eat can be very different. In the southeast, Cantonese food is prepared using relatively few spices, and is usually stir-fried or steamed. Chicken and pork is served with rice. In central China in the Szechwan and Hunan regions, the food is typically very spicy and hot. In eastern China, seafood is the basis of many meals. In northern China, meals tend to have lamb and pork, noodles, and steamed buns filled with meat. Cooks use only the freshest ingredients. Chefs are proud of dishes that look beautiful in terms of color, arrangement, and texture. Food display at top restaurants is an art and just as important as the balance of flavors and taste, and the yin-yang balance of hot and cold properties of food in the digestive system.

Did you know that emperors in the Tang Dynasty enjoyed buffalo milk mixed with flour and put in metal cans to freeze in a pool of ice—just like ice cream? Historians also believe Emperor Qin enjoyed frozen rice and milk in about 200 BCE—over 2,200 years ago!

Dining Etiquette: Dos and Don'ts

- Take your shoes off when entering a home, to help it stay clean.
- It is ok to drink soup out of a bowl, and hold a rice bowl near your lips as you eat your rice.
- Do not point your chopsticks or the spout of a teapot at someone.
- Do not lick your chopsticks, and do not let your chopsticks touch your tongue or lips if you are using them to take food from a group serving dish.
- If using your chopsticks to serve food, use the thick ends that did not touch your mouth.
- It is polite to keep your neighbor's tea cup filled.

- Do not cut noodles because this means you will have a shortened life.
- Do not stab your food with chopsticks, or let your chopsticks stand upright in your rice.
- When you are a guest at someone's home or at a restaurant in China, learn how to give compliments to the chef without suggesting you want more food. If you praise the food, more food will be put in front of you. It is wise to leave a small amount of food on your plate, so your host will not think you are leaving hungry.

How to Use Chopsticks

With the proper hand position and a little practice, you can learn to eat with chopsticks! Follow these steps:

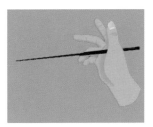

Step 1
Hold the thick end of one chopstick between the base of your thumb and your hand. Rest the thin end on the tips of your last two fingers, which should be slightly curved. This chopstick will stay still.

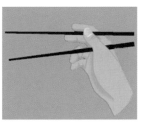

Step 2
Then take the other chopstick and hold it between the tips of your first two fingers and tip of your thumb. Curve your fingers.

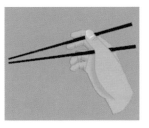

Step 3
To pick something up, move the top chopstick up and down.

First, try practicing with chunky pieces of food, like marshmallows or pieces of popcorn. Then, as you become more comfortable, you'll be able to pick up pieces of meat, vegetables, or lumps of sticky rice!

Chinese Beliefs 中国人的信仰

ike in ancient Greece and Rome, there are many gods and goddesses in Chinese folklore. All the major religions of the world are practiced in China. In addition, Confucianism and Taoism are ideas that China contributed to the world. They influence daily life even now.

⊙ Here are a few important Chinese gods and goddesses (clockwise, from top left): Cai Shen, God of Prosperity; top right, Shou Xing, God of Longevity and Old Age. At the bottom left and right are the two door gods called Menshen. They help kids get peaceful sleep and guard against nightmares. In the center is Guan Yin, Goddess of Compassion and Healing. As the female Buddha, she is also known as a Protector of Children.

Confucius
Kong Fu Zi (Confucius), who lived from 551 to 479 BCE, taught many rules for correct living, social behavior, and respect for order. Called the "Supreme Sage," most people know him by his Latin name, Confucius. Men educated in Confucian values became advisors to emperors. His disciples compiled *The Analects* to summarize his teachings. Here is a sample:
• Every person can know what is right and wrong, and live by it.
• Everyone has his or her place in society and in the family.
• People in authority must be trained for their job before hiring, so the emperor could trust their work—an idea followed by government and businesses today.
Sadly, Kong Fu Zi's teachings did not value women as equal to men. For centuries, it was nearly impossible for girls to go to school, so their choices in society were limited. ⊙

○ **Temple festivals**
Can you spot the swirling ribbons of the dancers on stilts? The fan dancers on stilts? The man selling pinwheels and the woman offering fruit on a stick? The comical characters in the center? Temple festivals, typically in or near Buddhist temples, are a favorite family activity. What do you imagine the children might buy?

○ **Lao Tze**
Lao Tze, who lived from 606 to 530 BCE, was a wise man who wrote the *Tao Te Ching,* a book about how to live. Among many things, he taught:
• There is a life force called qi (chi), which is an energy in our bodies and in the environment around us.
• Living simply, "going with the flow" within ourselves and with nature, is the best way to find peace.
• Life and nature are always changing, due to the flow of life's energy, which can be experienced and felt.
• War is wrong—killing the life force of others should make people feel sad, not victorious.

Yin and Yang are symbols representing the balance and harmony of life. The Chinese believe that opposites create balance—that is, yin and yang. This concept comes from the teachings of Lao Tze. Yin includes "female" energy, such as earth, dark, cold, and sweet. Yang includes "male" energy, such as sky, light, heat, and sour. Remember the Chinese creation story, in which the world started out as a jumble of yin and yang (page 12)?

These concepts flow throughout all of Chinese culture, including medicine, martial arts, feng shui, and nutrition. One example is cooking. Do you love "hot and sour" soup, or "sweet and sour" pork? Many dishes are created to have a balance of taste, appearance and healing properties, one of many ways that yin and yang concepts are used.

Everyone has both yin and yang in them. This symbol shows how they are intertwined and balance.

Chinese Zodiac Animals
十二生肖动物

Did you know that Cat and Rat used to be best friends? How, and why, did they become fierce enemies?

The emperor explained the zodiac contest to the animals.

About 4,600 years ago, Emperor Huang Di wanted to create the first monthly calendar that would repeat every twelve years. All the animals in the kingdom were invited to a race. Only the first twelve animals would have a year named after them—a great honor!

To win a place in the zodiac, they had to run a long way, and then cross a fast-moving river. Cat and Rat were best friends, but not good swimmers! So, how did Rat win the race? Being the smallest animals, Cat and Rat jumped on the back of friendly Ox. Rat dangled a carrot in front of Ox to remind him of his reward for reaching the shore first. But when they were crossing, wily Rat tricked Cat by telling her there was a tasty fish swimming near Ox, then pushed Cat into the water!

When Ox reached the river's edge, Rat jumped on to the ground first, and won the race! So Ox came second, Tiger was third, Rabbit came fourth by hopping on river logs and stones to get across the river because rabbits are also poor swimmers. Mighty Dragon came fifth as he was late because he had taken time to make rain for a good harvest. Next came galloping Horse, with sneaky Snake wrapped around its leg. Following Horse came Sheep, then Monkey and Rooster, who found a raft to take them across the river. Their combined effort pleased the Emperor. The eleventh animal was Dog. Even though Dog was clearly a fast runner and swimmer, he stopped to take a nap, and nearly missed the race altogether! And the last animal? Little Pig swam across the river and became the twelfth animal of the zodiac.

The sopping wet and very angry Cat was left out of the zodiac, and very mad at Rat for pushing her into the water. This is how Cat and Rat went from being best friends to worst enemies for all time!

How Chinese Families Use the Zodiac Signs

The zodiac signs are a personal guide to help determine success in life and compatibility with other people. Here are some uses:

• Picking the birth year for children to be born
• Choosing compatible spouses
• Fitting a personality with an occupation

The Chinese calendar is an ancient lunar calendar, based on the cycles of the moon. It is a twelve-year calendar, one year for each of the twelve animals in the zodiac that you see here.

It is considered such an honor to be born in the year of the dragon that birthrates for these years go up! In 1976, 1988, and 2012 there were increases, but in 2000, there was a very large jump in Chinese children born in the millennium year. Expect another jump in 2024!

Rat 鼠
Optimistic, social, generous, frugal
1936, 1948, 1960, 1972, 1984, 1996, 2008, 2020

Ox 牛
Confident, leader, stubborn, smart
1937, 1949, 1961, 1973, 1985, 1997, 2009, 2021

Tiger 虎
Independent, bold, loving, sensitive
1938, 1950, 1962, 1974, 1986, 1998, 2010, 2022

Rabbit 兔
Kind, talented, respected, fortunate
1939, 1951, 1963, 1975, 1987, 1999, 2011, 2023

Dragon 龙
Intelligent, brave, successful, honest
1940, 1952, 1964, 1976, 1988, 2000, 2012, 2024

Snake 蛇
Wise, charming, deep thinker, helpful
1941, 1953, 1965, 1977, 1989, 2001, 2013, 2025

Horse 马
Independent, hard working, friendly
1942, 1954, 1966, 1978, 1990, 2002, 2014, 2026

Sheep 羊
Shy, creative, gentle, elegant, sensitive
1943, 1955, 1967, 1979, 1991, 2003, 2015, 2027

Monkey 猴
Clever, well-liked, fast learner, impatient
1944, 1956, 1968, 1980, 1992, 2004, 2016, 2028

Rooster 鸡
Honest, bold, hard working, smart
1945, 1957, 1969, 1981, 1993, 2005, 2017, 2029

Dog 狗
Loyal, responsible, deep sense of justice
1946, 1958, 1970, 1982, 1994, 2006, 2018, 2030

Pig 猪
Sincere, smart, courageous, friend for life
1947, 1959, 1971, 1983, 1995, 2007, 2019, 2031

Ancient Chinese Arts Are Alive Today

Martial Arts 武术

Tai chi and kung fu are the "grandfathers" of the world's martial arts. These come in many different forms to channel qi, the body's energy, and build strength, speed, and balance. Karate, tae kwon do, and jujitsu, are just some examples that evolved in other Asian countries.

Kung fu 功夫

Testing one's power, energy and grace, kung fu (also known as wu shu and gong fu) combines self defense and performance art. Buddhist monks developed many different styles—some are based on the movements of tigers, monkeys, snakes, and even praying mantises, cranes, and dragons. Kung fu builds strength, speed, and quick reflexes. It expands and channels the body's energy and life force, resulting in great focus and body control.

Guan Yu, God of Martial Arts, wanted these skills to be used to avoid confrontation. He was peace loving, using his powers to defeat enemies by disarming them, not killing them. ◯

◯ Tai chi 太极

The illustration above shows a complete tai chi movement. Doesn't it look both energizing and peaceful? Tai chi is gentle movement with health benefits for all ages. All across China, people start their day with this graceful, meditative exercise, sometimes called shadow boxing. You can see children, parents, and grandparents practicing tai chi in parks, school grounds, and in front of the factories in which they work. Look for tai chi classes in your community.

Can you sense the energy jump off the page as these martial artists fly through the air?

Traditional Chinese Medicine 传统中医治疗

How do Chinese people stay healthy? In China and many parts of Asia with large Chinese populations, most hospitals and doctors offer both Traditional Chinese Medicine (TCM) and Western medicine. Most Chinese use TCM and herbal treatments before going to physicians.

Herbs that heal are used by TCM providers, as well as meditation and qi gong to help in the healing process. Qi gong focuses on releasing negative energy (sickness) and bringing in positive, healing energy. Like tai chi, qi gong movements are very slow, deliberate, and flowing.

Acupressure and acupuncture open blockages and restore the flow of energy in the body. An acupressurist uses both deep and gentle pressure massage techniques along the body's meridians, or pathways, to allow healing energy to flow to the heart, lungs, and other organs. Acupuncture and acupressure are widely accepted as effective forms of healing in most countries.

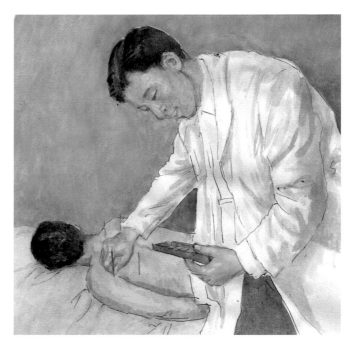

○ An acupuncturist inserts needles with tiny points along the meridians which seem blocked. You can hardly feel when the needles go in—surprisingly, it really does not hurt!

Based upon ideas from Lao Tze and others, Traditional Chinese Medicine teaches that qi—the body's energy and life force—needs to find its way, to flow easily like water in a mountain stream. It is thought that acupuncture began over 2,000 years ago, as medical men figured out that qi moves along pathways called meridians that connect the body's organs. Illness blocks the flow of this life energy, like a dam in a mountain stream. Treatment means unblocking the little dams on these pathways so the energy-filled blood flows to fight the illness. In the process the balance of yin and yang is restored. There are more than 800 "acu-points" that can be treated for blockages, although most treatments use less than a dozen.

○ The earliest surviving book on Chinese herbs was produced about 2,000 years ago. A modern herbalist knows about 6,000 substances, most of which are plant based—a few are minerals and animal parts. Herbal medicine is often made as a tea or a soup, but some can be dried, ground up, and made into pills or creams.

The Chinese Language

Mandarin is the official language of China. There are many other dialects such as Cantonese, Shanghaiese or Toisan, which are used in China, and in other countries that are home to people of Chinese origin, such as Malaysia, Vietnam, and Singapore. Chinese characters do not change with the dialect, so people can always read Chinese writing, even if they do not know the dialect.

Try saying some common word and phrases:

ENGLISH	MANDARIN PINYIN
Hello	**Nǐhǎo** 你好
Good job/Well done!	**Hěnhǎo** 很好
Thank you	**Xièxie** 谢谢
You are welcome	**Bùkèqi** 不客气
No thank you	**Bùyào, xièxie** 不要，谢谢
My name is _____.	**Wǒ shì** 我是 _____。
What is your name?	**Nǐ shì?** 你是？

Counting in Pinyin

0	零	**líng**	11	十一	**shíyī**	21	二十一	**èrshíyī**
1	一	**yī**	12	十二	**shíèr**	30	三十	**sānshí**
2	二	**èr**	13	十三	**shísān**	31	三十一	**sānshíyī**
3	三	**sān**	14	十四	**shísì**	40	四十	**sìshí**
4	四	**sì**	15	十五	**shíwǔ**	50	五十	**wǔshí**
5	五	**wǔ**	16	十六	**shíliù**	60	六十	**liùshí**
6	六	**liù**	17	十七	**shíqī**	70	七十	**qīshí**
7	七	**qī**	18	十八	**shíbā**	80	八十	**bāshí**
8	八	**bā**	19	十九	**shíjiǔ**	90	九十	**jiǔshí**
9	九	**jiǔ**	20	二十	**èrshí**	100	一百	**yìbǎi**
10	十	**shí**						

Did you know that Chinese women developed their own written language in the Qing Dynasty? In central China, they created a secret language used to write letters, decorate fans and handkerchiefs, and weave messages into clothes. Because women were denied schooling, and many had bound feet (meaning it was painful to walk), this was a way to privately communicate with other women. It was called *nu-shu*, meaning "women's writing."

Lucky Numbers

Traditionally, Chinese people believed in lucky numbers, and many still do today. The luckiest number is 8, because it sounds like "prosperity" in Chinese.

Many Chinese go to great lengths to have 8 in their phone number and address. Just as 8 is lucky, some consider 4 unlucky, as the word sounds like "death" in Chinese. However, there are positive associations with 4, as well as other numbers:

- Three (**sān** 三) for three plenties—happiness, many children, and a long life
- Four (**sì** 四) for the four seasons and four seas
- Five (**wǔ** 五) for five happinesses—luck, prosperity, longevity, happiness, and wealth
- Six (**liù** 六) sounds like things will go well/smooth sailing
- Eight in Chinese (**bā** 八) sounds like the word for prosperity, and as a number which mirrors itself, it represents ideal balance
- Nine (**jiǔ** 九) sounds like the word for "longevity." The Forbidden City had 90 palaces, 9,999 rooms for 9,000 people living there!
- Do you remember that the 2008 Olympics in China began at 8:08 pm on 8-8-08 (August 8, 2008)?

Say It in Chinese

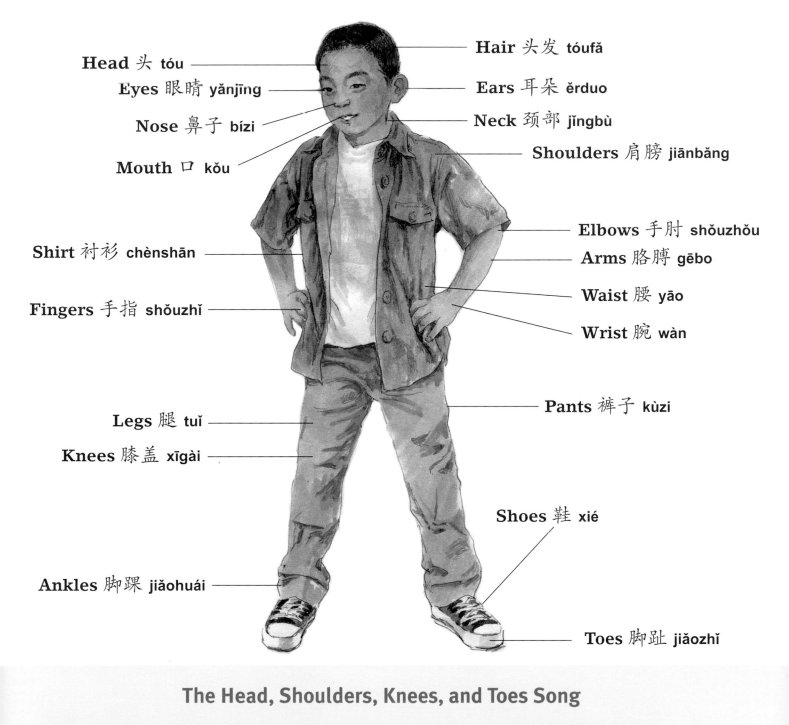

Head 头 tóu

Eyes 眼睛 yǎnjīng

Nose 鼻子 bízi

Mouth 口 kǒu

Hair 头发 tóufǎ

Ears 耳朵 ěrduo

Neck 颈部 jǐngbù

Shoulders 肩膀 jiānbǎng

Elbows 手肘 shǒuzhǒu

Arms 胳膊 gēbo

Waist 腰 yāo

Wrist 腕 wàn

Shirt 衬衫 chènshān

Fingers 手指 shǒuzhǐ

Pants 裤子 kùzi

Legs 腿 tuǐ

Knees 膝盖 xīgài

Shoes 鞋 xié

Ankles 脚踝 jiǎohuái

Toes 脚趾 jiǎozhǐ

The Head, Shoulders, Knees, and Toes Song

Tóu jiān bǎng xī gài jiǎo xī gài jiǎo zhǐ
Head, shoulders, knees and toes, knees and toes
头 肩 膀 膝 盖 脚 膝 盖 脚 趾

Tóu jiān bǎng xī gài jiǎo xī gài jiǎo zhǐ
Head, shoulders, knees and toes, knees and toes
头 肩 膀 膝 盖 脚 膝 盖 脚 趾

Yǎn jīng ěr duo kǒu bí zi Tóu jiān bǎng xī gài jiǎo pài pài shǒu
eyes and ears and mouth and nose Head, shoulders, knees and toes clap your hands
眼 睛 耳 朵 口 鼻 子 头 肩 膀 膝 盖 脚 拍 拍 手

41

Selected Chinese Arts and Crafts

⊕ This maginificent jade carving of a sailing ship is about 10 feet (3 meters) tall. How tall is the young girl?

⊕ This hollow glass bottle was painted from the inside using special right-angle brushes.

⊕ Cloisonné is a style of decoration that melts metal and colorful enamel together.

⊕ ⊕ Why are these porcelain bowls called "egg shell" pottery? They are as light as eggshells and you can see through the tiny, rice grain-sized windows!

⊕ A paper cut lantern.

⊕ This elaborate knot is a classic wall decoration for Chinese New Year.

Use Calligraphy to Make Your Own Card

Holding a paintbrush as shown (right), try writing a few well-known characters and sayings. Make greeting cards for your friends and family.

Try Chinese brush painting by experimenting with different strokes, different amounts of ink, and pressure on the brush. Create simple pictures using the steps shown. Then make your own special cards for friends and family using the characters below. Add color to the final picture on the card.

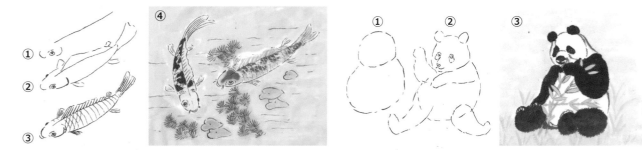

✿ Brush painting is a beautiful art that takes years to master, but everyone starts at the beginning! Using the steps shown above, try holding the paint brush, try the brush strokes, and then create simple pictures. Make handpainted cards for special occasions using these paintings. Practice writing one of the three greetings below, then add it to the card for a family member or friend. The stroke order is shown at the end of each completed stroke.

✿ Greeting card text examples with brushstrokes. To make your own card, copy one of the three greetings (right).

✿ Happy Birthday   ✿ Happy New Year   ✿ Good Fortune

Chinese Music, Dance, and Theater

Classical Chinese music sounds quite different from Western music, as it is based on the five-tone scale, compared to Western music's eight-tone scale. Along with the Chinese gong and drums, the instruments below have been making beautiful music for centuries.

◐ Music

Musicians play inside the stunningly beautiful hall at the Heavenly Palace, also called the Temple of Heaven. Left to right: Two *erhus*, *yangqin*, *dizi*, *guzheng*, *pipa*, and *ruan*.

- The *erhu* only has two strings, but its sweet, expressive tone can sound like a violin or viola. It came into China about a thousand years ago from tribes north of China.
- The *yangqin* is a hammered dulcimer: the player hits the strings with a small stick or mallet. *Yangqins* originated in Persia and made their way to China via the Silk Road during the Ming Dynasty.
- The *dizi* is the Chinese bamboo flute, which is known to have been used in China for at least 2,000 years.
- The *guzheng* is a long, plucked instrument that is thought to have been in China since 350 BCE. Its beautiful, lyrical tone makes it a perfect solo instrument. Some say the strings sound like flowing water when they are struck consecutively.
- The *pipa* is a four-stringed lute that looks like a pear. It also dates back over 3,000 years and is used both in orchestra performances, as well as solos.
- The *ruan* is moon-shaped, with a short neck and four strings. Called the Chinese guitar, it dates back to at least the Qin Dynasty. It is used in Chinese opera and modern music.

Chinese opera

Traditional Chinese opera, which began in the Song Dynasty (960–1279), is a fantastic, imaginative retelling of familiar folk stories and historical events. Still popular today, it mixes singing, dancing, poetry, martial arts, acrobatics, and above all, colorful costumes and masks. ○

○ Chinese opera masks

The faces of the characters are meant to show their emotions, like passion, love, anger, aggression, and other strong feelings. Chinese opera masks were usually painted on the face or painted on cloth or ceramic masks worn over the face.

Mask of the mischievious Monkey King

○ Dance

Chinese folk dancing goes back hundreds, perhaps thousands of years. The movement of hands and feet expressed appreciation for life, to the gods for plentiful crops, and to act out scenes from everyday life. Dancers are often athletic and incorporate eye-popping acrobatic or martial arts moves. Common folk dances include dancing with colorful ribbons and fans, acting out stories from the Chinese zodiac, folk tales and folk songs.

All the Chinese minority groups have distinctive dances that reflect the hopes, dreams, challenges, and lifestyles of that group. China's thousands of folk dances are part of its colorful cultural heritage.

Below, dozens of dancers line up behind one another in the dance, "Guan Yin with One Thousand Hands."

Get a plain face mask at a

crafts store, along with paints made to go on that mask. Use these masks to inspire you, and have fun making your own Chinese opera mask!

Guan Yu mask (left); Zhang Fei mask (right)

Important Festivals and Holidays

○ **Dragon dance**
Chinese dragons are kind, powerful, and protective—very different from the ferocious and aggressive dragons of European myths. The dragon is a sacred animal, and an emblem that emperors had woven into their clothes. During the festival, the dragon welcomes the New Year, and wishes everyone good fortune and peace. All over the world, the Chinese dragon is seen as a kind, friendly, strong, and courageous creature that brings good things to good people.

Chinese New Year 农历新年

Chinese New Year is the biggest, most important festival in China. People travel great distances to be with their families. Many businesses close. Using a lunar calendar, festivities begin with a family reunion on New Year's Eve before the first day of the first month of the New Year (usually in February), and go on for two weeks. Fantastic Chinese New Year parades happen in cities around the world.

Chinese New Year, also called Spring Festival, marks the end of winter and new beginnings. Many customs are followed, which include hoping for good fortune, a successful harvest, and good health to all. Lively markets sell flowers and fruit, especially fruit that is gold or red in color, like mandarin oranges, pomelos, kumquats, apples, and persimmons. Gold represents abundance and red is for happiness. These become gifts and are used in homes, at temple altars, and during meals. People exchange plants to symbolize rebirth and new growth for the coming year.

Did you know that the dragon was born from the imagination of people? It has a camel's head, a deer's antlers, a lobster's eyes, an ox's ears, an eagle's claws, a goat's beard, a snake's long body, the belly of a frog, and it is covered with fish scales (a symbol of plenty).

Nián and the Chinese New Year
How did the Chinese New Year start?

According to Chinese legend, the beginning of Chinese New Year started with a fight against a monster called the Nián.

The Nián would come on the last day of the lunar New Year to devour livestock, crops, and even villagers, especially children. To protect the villagers and their property, the people put food for this scary creature in front of their doors at the end of every year. They hoped that if the Nián ate the food they had prepared, it would stop attacking people. They wanted the Nián to be full, so it would not eat their animals and crops.

One time, people saw that the Nián was scared away by a little child wearing a red coat. The villagers then understood that the Nián was afraid of the color red. After that, just before each New Year, the villagers would hang red lanterns and red scrolls on windows and doors. People also used firecrackers to frighten away the Nián. From then on, the scary Nián never came to the village again.

What do you say to someone at Chinese New Year?

The most common greeting is "Gōng Xǐ, Gōng Xǐ," or "Gōng Xǐ Fā Cái." Gōng Xǐ literally means, "We are happy that you got through the last year," and Fā Cái means, "Wishing you to strike it rich in the coming year." Other common Mandarin sayings are "Xīn Nián Kuài Lè," or "Xīn Nián Hǎo," which mean "Happy New Year."

Zao Jun, the spirit of the Kitchen God, watches over the cooking.

◔ The Kitchen God

Just like some people believe Santa Claus checks to see if you have been naughty or nice, the Chinese believe that just before New Year's Eve, the Kitchen God sends a report to the Jade Emperor about everyone's behavior.

To prepare, people get haircuts and new clothes, families do "spring cleaning" and paint their home, bring in flowers and fresh golden fruits, pay bills, and clear up old disagreements that could bring bad feelings into the New Year.

Nearly all cooking is done days in advance, as New Year's Day is meant to be a day of rest. On New Year's Eve, a special feast is prepared, and everyone gathers at the family home. Chinese kids all over the world stay up to welcome in the New Year. Some people believe that the later the kids stay up, the longer their parents will live!

New Year's offerings
Offerings of thanks are made to the ancestors at the family altar, especially for the New Year. ◔

On New Year's Day people dress in new clothes, and, on their best behavior, visit friends and family with gifts of sweets and fruit. Children receive money in red envelopes from their parents and adult relatives as a New Year gift. Pomelos symbolize blessings, while tangerines and oranges mean good luck and prosperity. These fruits are left with their leaves intact, to represent families and friends staying together. Most importantly, offerings of thanks are made to the ancestors at the family altar.

On the second day of the New Year, family visits are returned with gifts of sweets and golden fruit. Pine and cypress branches are put in a vase, and decorated with old coins, paper flowers, and charms. This is a traditional "money tree"—a wish for prosperity in the New Year.

Sweets are served to family and friends on a Harmony Tray, arranged in either groups of nine, which sounds like "longevity," or eight, which sounds like "prosperity." Some popular items on a Harmony Tray include candied melon (for growth and good health), red melon seeds (for joy, happiness, truth, many sons, and sincerity), candied coconut (for togetherness), and lotus seeds (for fertility).

◔ **The Chinese New Year Banquet**
Look at all the delicious food! Fish, noodles, duck, green vegetables, and more! This family is really enjoying being together for a Chinese New Year's Eve feast. Look for these traditions:
• The character for good fortune, 福 fú, is hung upside down, to mean luck has arrived and will stay in the home!
• The red banners, called chunlian, hold poems with good wishes for the new year.
• The family is eating at a round table shaped like the moon, symbolizing family unity.

Special Chinese New Year Recipes (4-6 servings each)

Kid-Friendly Long Life Noodles

Ingredients
1 lb fresh Asian-style long life noodles,
  either rice or wheat (Don't cut the noodles!)
1½ teaspoons hoisin sauce
½ teaspoon cornstarch
2 tablespoons dark soy sauce
1 tablespoon low sodium soy sauce
1 teaspoon sugar
1 tablespoon oil
½ teaspoon garlic, minced
½ cup finely diagonally sliced green onions
(Optional: Add ½ cup peanut butter in step 2)

Directions
1. Cook noodles according to package directions, without oil and salt. Rinse with cold water, drain, and set aside.
2. Combine all remaining ingredients, except green onions, in a small bowl. Stir until mixed.
3. Add mixture to noodles while gently stirring.
4. Sprinkle green onions on top of noodles and serve either hot or cold.

Soy Sauce and Ginger Chicken

Ingredients
1 large whole chicken
8 large cloves of garlic
1–2 tablespoons peeled, *sliced* fresh ginger,
  plus 1 teaspoon peeled and *diced* fresh ginger
3 tablespoons soy sauce
1 tablespoon rice vinegar
½ to 1 teaspoon chili oil, to taste
green onions (scallions) or coriander leaves
(cilantro) for garnish

Directions
1. Boil 5 quarts of water in large pot with 5 cloves of garlic and *sliced* ginger.
2. Put the whole chicken in the water, return to boil, and simmer for 1 hour.
3. Drain, cool, remove skin (optional), and cut chicken into pieces.
4. Finely crush the remaining garlic and *diced* ginger. Add soy sauce, vinegar, and chili oil to form a marinade.
5. Toss the chicken pieces in the marinade and keep in refrigerator at least 2 hours before serving.

Auntie Lili's Festive Almond or Mango Jello

Ingredients
3 tablespoons Knox unflavored gelatin
1 cup sugar
1 tablespoon almond extract
5 cups milk
(Optional: mangos or mandarin orange slices
for serving)

Directions
1. Mix the gelatin into 1 cup of cold water.
2. Boil the sugar in 3 cups of water until it dissolves,
   then pour it into the gelatin mixture.
3. Add the almond extract and milk. Stir well.*
4. Pour the mixture into serving size bowls or a jello mold.
5. Refrigerate overnight.
7. If using, serve with sliced mangos or mandarin oranges.

○ Serving suggestion: The center of
the plate contains the mango jello,
with almond jello surrounding it. A
small cupcake baking pan was used
as a mold for the almond jello.

*To make mango jello, add 2 cups of pureed mango before step 4.

Did you know that the character for
"abundance" (yu) sounds the same as the
character for "fish"? That is why fish dishes
form the centerpiece of the New Year's Eve
feast. The whole fish, including the head, is
served pointed toward the guest of honor or
head of the household. Other auspicious foods
served are:

• Long life noodles, which should never be cut,
  so as to avoid bad luck.

• Special preparations of green vegetables (green is the color of wealth and shared prosperity).

• Dumplings are considered very lucky, as eating them signifies a large and prosperous family.
  Some cooks add a lucky coin to the dumplings.

• Dessert is often sweet, round rice balls, in the shape of the moon, a perfect symbol for family
  unity and reunion. Yummy almond or mango jello is also a special treat.

Chinese New Year Gifts

One of the best parts of Chinese New Year is that parents, grandparents, aunties, and uncles and other adult friends give kids money, sealed in bright red envelopes called *hong bao* (Mandarin) or *lai see* (Cantonese).

○ How to Give Gifts

Gifts should be wrapped in red or bright colors: avoid white, the color of death. Do not open gifts in front of the giver, to sidestep possible embarrassment to the gift giver. When exchanging gifts, use both hands to offer the gift and two hands to receive it. Traditionally, this act is done while bowing slightly, which means, "you are important to me."

Chinese New Year Crafts

The Red Envelope 红包封

Common symbols on the red envelopes are the characters for good luck, or the zodiac animal for the New Year (see page 37). Using bright red paper, cut out, paste, and fold your red envelope along the fold lines shown left; then, using gold foil paper, draw, cut out and paste on the decoration you would like for your *hong bao*! Shown here is the character for good fortune.

A Chinese New Year Lantern 灯笼

This cutting pattern can also be used for Autumn Moon Festival.

Materials

2 pcs. construction paper; scissors; glue, tape or stapler; crayons or markers; Chinese tassle or curling ribbon

Steps

1. Draw your own design on paper.
2. Fold in half, lengthwise; then fold back 1 inch (2.5 cm) along both long horizontal edges.
3. Cut slits about ¾ inch (2 cm) apart.
4. Open and tape the 1 inch (2.5 cm) fold backs together to form the top and bottom of lantern.
5. Insert a second piece of paper, rolled up, inside lantern to stabilize. Maybe use a contrasting color.
6. Tape or staple inside paper to lantern.
7. Tape or staple a red cord or ribbon at top for handle.
8. Add red ribbons or Chinese tassle to bottom.

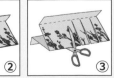

The Lion Dance 舞狮

Can you hear the drums beating? Firecrackers popping? Chinese New Year parades are full of excitement as the lions dip and prance down the street shaking their heads to the beat of the drums. Last in the parade is the long silky dragon, dancing as the exploding firecrackers light up the sky, wishing everyone good fortune!

What is a lion made of? It has the soft body of a lion, the shaggy fur of a lion, the eyes of a rabbit, the antlers of a deer, the ears of a dog, the antenna of a dragonfly, the paws of a tiger, the horn of a rhino, and the beard of a billy goat!

Lion dances combine detailed movement with specific musical rhythms. The Chinese believe evil spirits move in straight lines, so the lion deliberately walks in a zigzag pattern to confuse the spirits. The two people inside the lion have special strings to open and close the lion's eyes and mouth while dancing, to give the lion more expressions. The lion's movements, together with the loud drumming, gongs, and cymbals, scare off evil spirits, along with traditional fireworks used outside. Other customary dances playfully beckon good fortune, prosperity, and a fine spring harvest. Billions, yes, billions of people enjoy Chinese New Year celebrations around the world.

Did you know lions came to China via the Silk Road in the Han Dynasty? Rulers from what are now Iran and Afghanistan gave lions to China's emperors to ensure their right to trade with Chinese merchants. Buddhists and many others believe the lion represents courage, energy, and wisdom. Most Chinese folktales show the lion as peaceful, unlike the fierce tiger native to the Middle Kingdom.

⭘ Since the beginning of time, people have dreamed of flying. Kites were one of our first successes in beating gravity. As early as 1080 BCE, the Chinese flew kites.

During Qing Ming, kites are flown as a way to reach up to the heavens and send good thoughts to those no longer alive. Children and their parents make their own kites in a long-standing tradition of families brought together by this ancient pleasure.

The Qing Ming Festival 清明节

Why is Qing Ming so important? Qing Ming (or Ching Ming) Festival literally means "Clear and Bright." It is a time to celebrate the coming of spring by remembering elders and ancestors. It honors long-standing family roots. Held on April 5th, it is the only major Chinese holiday on the Western calendar.

People visit the graves of their ancestors, share fond memories, and pay respects to loved ones. This includes freshening the graves by sweeping away any dust and mud, pulling off weeds, and bringing fresh flowers and golden fruit to lay on the graves. Meals are often served in celebration and in honor of grandparents, great grandparents, and those from earlier generations.

Qing Ming is a way to celebrate the arrival of spring, love of family, and in particular those who inspire and guide us from the heavens.

The Dragon Boat Festival 端午节

The Dragon Boat Festival is usually held on the fifth day of the fifth month, around early to mid June. Known also as Double Fifth, this festival celebrates the life of a wise man named Qu Yuan (340–278 BCE) who was a government official and statesman. He was admired by people for battling corruption. Dishonest officials forced the emperor to have him removed from his post and sent away into exile, where he became a famous poet. This holiday became a way to commemorate Qu Yuan's noble character.

◑ Can you hear the swoosh of the oars in the water? The drum beats that help the rowers keep time? On rivers, lakes, and bays all over China and in many parts of Asia, brightly decorated dragon boats compete for the honor of winning the race. Each boat carries 14–20 rowers, a drummer with a powerful voice who creates the rhythm for the rowers to follow, and a person who steers. Before the race, there is a ceremony to bring the elaborately carved dragon to life by painting its eyes. From the nearby shore, people cheer on their favorite team.

◑ The favorite food for this festival time is *zongzi*, a packet made of glutinous rice mixed with meats and wrapped in bamboo leaves. *Zongzi* can be made as salty, sweet or spicy, and hot or cold. Sometimes called the Chinese tamale, people enjoy eating *zongzi* while watching hundreds of boats compete, rowing to the thunderous rhythms of the many drums.

The Autumn Moon Festival 中秋节

Celebrated under a bright, full moon in September, the Autumn Moon Festival is to reunite spiritually with loved ones who are no longer with us, like Chang'e and her beloved Hou Yi (page 56). It is also a time to send good thoughts to those who are far away, but who can look up at the same bright moon, and think of us, too. The moon's circular shape symbolizes family unity and love. This festival also celebrates a good harvest, and a time to enjoy moon cakes with family and friends, in honor of the Moon Goddess. Legend has it that mooncakes were used for military purposes. The Yuan Dynasty Chinese who did not like their Mongolian rulers put messages in mooncakes containing orders to defeat the emperor's army. Some say this led to the overthrow of the Yuan Dynasty and the beginning of the Ming Dynasty.

How Chang'e Became a Moon Goddess 嫦娥奔月的传说

Long ago, ten suns circled the Earth. One day, all ten suns appeared at once, scorching our planet and causing a horrible drought. A brave archer named Hou Yi was summoned to help solve the problem. His arrows shot down all but one of these suns, and the Earth was saved. As his reward, the Heavenly Queen Mother gave Hou Yi a special Potion of Immortality.

"If you drink this special potion, you will live forever. But you must use it wisely," said the Heavenly Queen Mother.

Hou Yi hid the potion, saving it to drink with his beautiful wife, Chang'e (Chong Erh). But, she accidentally found it. Curious, she took a few sips of its sweet nectar. To her surprise, she began to feel lightheaded, and then ... she began to rise up in the air and drifted toward the moon, where she lives to this day.

Feeling sorry for Chang'e in her loneliness, the Heavenly Queen Mother gave Chang'e a beautiful, white jade rabbit to keep her company. When Hou Yi came home and saw what had happened, his heart was broken.

"My beautiful wife is gone! We cannot share our lives forever!" he cried.

For the rest of his days, he would look up at the moon and think about the lovely Chang'e living there. And thus began the legend of the beautiful woman in the moon—the Moon Goddess. And if you look up at the bright, round moon during the Autumn Moon Festival, you just might see the beautiful Chang'e and her white jade rabbit!

A Simple Kid-Friendly Mooncake Recipe
最简单的月饼制作方法

Sweet red or black bean paste is a typical filling Chinese filling; some non-Chinese children may prefer jam.

Ingredients
1 tube crescent dinner roll dough
1 tablespoon butter, melted
½ cup sweet red or black bean paste, or a jam such as strawberry, apricot, or raspberry

Directions
1. Preheat your oven according to package directions.
2. Unroll the triangular sheets of dough.
3. Place 1 teaspoon of jam or bean paste in the center.
4. Roll up the dough, according to package directions, and tuck the ends underneath.
5. Brush the rolls with the melted butter.
6. Bake according to package instructions.
7. Cool for 20 minutes and enjoy!

⬆ Traditional mooncakes always have designs printed on them, created by pressing them into carved molds, and then baking them. Sweet mooncakes are filled with bean paste, lotus seed paste, or egg yolks. Savory mooncakes contain nuts and meats. Both are very rich foods, and meant to be shared!

Endangered Species and Environments in Peril

Endangered species in China include the giant panda, golden monkey, South China tiger, Siberian tiger, Asian elephant, black-necked crane, crested ibis, Yangtze River dolphin, certain sharks, and many others. Animals can become endangered when people build houses, mine, or log trees on the land where the animals live, eat, and mate. The animals then have no place to live. Or sometimes wildlife poachers kill the animals to sell body parts, like fur, tusks, and shark fins for wearing or eating. Pollution and climate change also make it harder for animals (and people!) to find clean water to drink and clean air to breathe, so some species have died off.

- There are more than 385 threatened species in China.
- Giant pandas lost half of their habitat between 1974 and 1989, so they had very little territory in which to live, eat, and mate.

What can you do to help endangered species? Learn about why it matters if a species becomes extinct. Look on the internet and get active in kid-friendly environmental groups, such as Roots and Shoots and Kids F.A.C.E. Talk with your friends, teachers, and parents and think about what you can do. (See Resources, page 61.)

● Pandas are the most famous of China's endangered species. They live in the mountains of Sichuan, Gansu, and Shaanxi provinces, and eastern Tibet. China runs a world-class research and breeding center in Wolong, Sichuan Province. Can you find this on page 6? Pandas mainly eat bamboo, plus a few small fish and rodents. Momma pandas can give birth once a year. Only about 1,600 giant pandas still live in the wild. At birth, they weigh 3–5 ounces (80–140g). At about three months old, this panda is about 10–12 pounds (4–5 kg), and still fits into the palm of a hand! A grown panda weighs 350 pounds (160 kg) or more.

● Golden monkeys live in the forests of Sichuan, Yunnan, and Guizhou. Their habitat is being lost to new building development and poachers, who can sell their fire-orange fur for a good price.

● South China tigers are one of the smaller breeds of tigers. They can be seen only in zoos, as they are almost extinct in the wild.

● Chang Jiang River dolphins (also known as the Yangtze River dolphin) may have recently become extinct.

⊙ This huge stone Buddha did not used to be brown and filthy! Air pollution has badly damaged it. This peaceful Buddha was carved out of a cliff in Leshan during the Tang Dynasty (618–907). It is 233 feet (71 meters) tall—about 20 stories high and is a UNESCO World Heritage site. Can you spot the hundreds of steps used to get to the bottom?

Everyone has heard of the Great Wall. But have you heard of the Great Green Wall? Nearly every spring, Beijing is blasted by terrible sandstorms that come from the Gobi Desert and plains of Inner Mongolia. Sand and dirt cover the city, sometimes even causing problems for nearby North and South Korea and Japan. To fix the problem, a Great Green Wall of tall forest trees is being planted to block the sand. The trees are growing, but will take many years, as the Great Green Wall is planned to be 2,800 miles (4,506 kilometers) long, about half as long as the Great Wall's 5,300 miles (8,530 kilometers).

China has very complicated environmental problems. Its industrial growth has been so fast, the legal systems that other industrialized countries have built up over centuries to protect the environment have not been put in place, especially in China's big urban areas. These include ways to reduce air pollution from traffic and factories, make sure drinking water is safe, and waste water from toilets and factories is treated to take out chemicals and bad bacteria before being recycled or going into groundwater systems. Reducing the amount of used plastic and electronic equipment is also a huge environmental challenge. China is working on these problems, but it will take time, and all of us working together.

Xie Xie! 谢谢!
Thank you for joining us on this journey to learn all about China!

Zai Jian! 再见!
We are the next generation! Remember to reduce, reuse, and recycle! What happens in China affects the whole world, and the opposite is also true. Think about what you can do to help!

Glossary

BCE   Before the Common Era, or all dates before the year 0 (also known as BC, or Before Christ)

CE   Common Era, or all dates after the year 0 (also known as AD).

Dynasty   Government by people in the same family. Chinese history is divided into periods based upon the reigns of ruling families.

Extended Families   Families that include not just parents and children, but also other relatives such as grandparents, aunties, uncles and/or cousins all living together in one home.

Lacquer   A natural paint-like material from the sap of lacquer trees. It seals out moisture, heat, acids, and bacteria and is used to protect and preserve wood, bamboo, silk, and other materials from decay.

Martial Arts   Specific systems and traditions of self defense, combat, and using energy.

Nomads   People who move around, carrying their homes and animals with them.

Porcelain   A thin, shiny, and delicate glazed pottery made from fine kaolin clay found in the mountains of China.

Terra Cotta   A hard, rough, and unglazed clay, usually reddish brown, which was used for early pottery, as well as small and large items to be put in tombs, like the Terra Cotta Warriors.

Traditional Chinese Medicine (TCM)   Refers primarily to acupressure, acupuncture, and healing with herbal, mineral, and animal medicines.

Opportunities for Action

A portion of the proceeds from this book will be donated to the following organizations that provide education, medical care, supportive living environments and child development training in orphanages in China. Readers and their families are encouraged to donate to, or volunteer in these, or similar non-profit organizations working in China:

Love Without Boundaries (www.lovewithoutboundaries.com) provides medical assistance, surgeries, and healing homes for medically needy orphans, as well as foster care, education, and nutrition assistance programs.

Half The Sky (www.halfthesky.org) provides model child development programs to orphanage workers across China. Caregivers are trained to provide intellectual, physical, and emotional stimulation to children in a nurturing environment, to help prepare them to fully participate in society when they are out of the orphanage.

Two organizations that offer children and teenagers opportunities to learn about, volunteer, and help fix environmental problems are:

Roots and Shoots (www.rootsandshoots.org), started by Dr. Jane Goodall to encourage young people around the world to get involved in environmental projects.

Kids For a Clean Environment (Kids F.A.C.E.—www.kidsface.org) has 2,000 chapters in 15 countries around the world, and is the world's largest youth environmental organization.

Resources

Books

Bowler, Ann Martin. *Adventures of the Treasure Fleet: China Discovers the World.* North Clarendon, VT: Tuttle Publishing, 2006.

Bridges, Shirin Yim. *Ruby's Wish.* San Francisco: Chronicle Books, 2002.

Cornue, Virginia, PhD. *The Dragon's Daughters Return.* Copper City, Michigan: Thimbleberry Press, 2007.

Demi. *Kites: Magic Wishes That Fly up to the Sky.* New York: Random House, 2006.

Ford, Barbara E. *The Master Revealed: A Journey with Tangrams.* Vallejo: Tandora's Box Press, 1988.

Han-Lin Chen, Danny. *An Introduction to Chinese Brush Painting* (kit). Richmond, British Columbia, Canada: Spicebox Publishing, 2007.

Krasno, Rena and Yeng-Fong Chiang. *Cloud Weavers: Ancient Chinese Legends.* Berkeley: Pacific View Press, 2003.

Lin, Grace. *Thanking the Moon: Celebrating the Mid Autumn Moon Festival.* New York: Random House, 2010.

Louis, Catherine. *My Little Book of Chinese Words.* New York: NorthSouth Books, 2006.

Major, John S. *The Silk Road.* New York: Harper Collins, 1996.

Man-Ho Kwok. *The Feng Shui Kit: The Chinese Way to Health, Wealth and Happiness at Home and at Work.* North Clarendon, VT: Tuttle Publishing, 1995.

Mann, Elizabeth. *The Great Wall.* New York: Mikaya Press, 1997.

Michaelson, Carol. *Ancient China.* New York: Time-Life Books, 1996.

Shemie, Bonnie. *Houses of China.* Toronto, Canada: Tundra Books, 1996.

Siyu Liu and Orel Protopopescu. *A Thousand Peaks: Poems from China.* Berkeley: Pacific View Press, 2002.

Steele, Philip. *Step into the Chinese Empire.* London: Anness Publishing, 2008.

Tan, Amy. *The Chinese Siamese Cat.* London: Macmillan Publishing Company, 1994.

Walters, Derek. *The Secrets of Chinese Astrology.* London: Hamlyn Publishing, 2003.

Wang Jian and Fang Xiaoyan. *An Illustrated Record of Chinese Civilization.* New York: Reader's Digest, 2009.

Zihong He. *My First Book of Chinese Calligraphy.* North Clarendon, VT: Tuttle Publishing, 2010.

Websites

Below is a sample of online catalogs for books, toys, games, language tools, cultural items, clothing, and more for children, teens, and adults:

Asia for Kids: www.afk.com
China Books and Periodicals: www.chinabooks.com
China Sprout: www.chinasprout.com
AJ Panda: www.ajpanda.com

Solutions to Tangram Puzzles

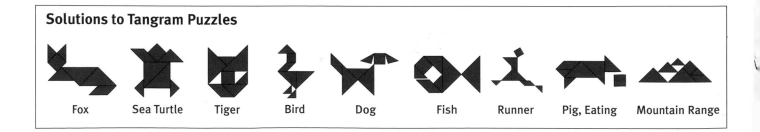

Fox   Sea Turtle   Tiger   Bird   Dog   Fish   Runner   Pig, Eating   Mountain Range

Index

Published by Tuttle Publishing, an imprint of
Periplus Editions (HK) Ltd.

www.tuttlepublishing.com

Library of Congress cataloging in process

ISBN 978-0-8048-4849-7
(Previously published with the ISBN 978-0-8048-4121-4)

Distributed by

North America, Latin America & Europe
Tuttle Publishing
364 Innovation Drive
North Clarendon, VT 05759-9436 U.S.A.
Tel: (802) 773-8930
Fax: (802) 773-6993
info@tuttlepublishing.com
www.tuttlepublishing.com

Japan
Tuttle Publishing
Yaekari Building, 3rd Floor
5-4-12 Osaki, Shinagawa-ku
Tokyo 141 0032
Tel: (81) 3 5437-0171
Fax: (81) 3 5437-0755
sales@tuttle.co.jp
www.tuttle.co.jp

Asia Pacific
Berkeley Books Pte. Ltd.
61 Tai Seng Avenue #02-12
Singapore 534167
Tel: (65) 6280-1330
Fax: (65) 6280-6290
inquiries@periplus.com.sg
www.periplus.com

First edition
20 19 18 17   10 9 8 7 6 5 4 3 2 1   1712EP
Printed in Hong Kong

ABOUT TUTTLE
"Books to Span the East and West"

Our core mission at Tuttle Publishing is to create books which bring people together one page at a time. Tuttle was founded in 1832 in the small New England town of Rutland, Vermont (USA). Our fundamental values remain as strong today as they were then—to publish best-in-class books informing the English-speaking world about the countries and peoples of Asia. The world has become a smaller place today and Asia's economic, cultural and political influence has expanded, yet the need for meaningful dialogue and information about this diverse region has never been greater. Since 1948, Tuttle has been a leader in publishing books on the cultures, arts, cuisines, languages and literatures of Asia. Our authors and photographers have won numerous awards and Tuttle has published thousands of books on subjects ranging from martial arts to paper crafts. We welcome you to explore the wealth of information available on Asia at **www.tuttlepublishing.com**.

Photo Credits

Dreamstime.com: **Margo555** 11; **Jianbinglee** 27 (*2nd from top*); **Camptoloma** 35; **Qushe** 39 (*top*); **Lai Ching Yuen** 42

iStock.com: **craft vision** 27 (*top*)

Robert Remen 45, 50 (*top and bottom*), 51 (*top*)

Shutterstock.com: **Robert F. Balazik** 4; **Mikrobiuz** 10 (*top*); **tcly** 10 (*2nd from top*); **feiyuezhangjie** 10 (*3rd from top*); **TonyV3112** 24; **Sinelyov** 33; **Lawrence Wee** 34; **fotohunter** 39 (*bottom*); **Chinaview** 47; **Hywit Dimyadi** 51 (*bottom*); **dolphfyn** 55

All other photos by **Allison Branscombe**